Unforgettable Finals

in

Champions League

History:

Champions League's Greatest Moments

By

Idobaba Jackson

TABLE OF CONTENTS

Introduction... 5

*The origin Champions League's..7

The Champions League's Unparalleled Drama.............. 14

*Real Madrid and AC Milan in the 1958 Clash of the Titans........ 21

*The impact of the Manchester United crash into the Munich Air Disaster on European... 24

*A memorable upset occurred in 1979 between Nottingham Forest and Malmo FF...............................30

Ajax vs. AC Milan (1995), The Dutch magnificent run................ 34

Juventus vs. Real Madrid (1998): Zidane's Magnificence................ 38

Manchester United's Late Heroes: The 1999 Matchup with Bayern Munich...42

Valencia vs. Real Madrid in The Spanish Showdown (2000)... 46

Real Madrid vs. Bayer Leverkusen (2002): Zinedine Zidane's Glorious Moment...49

Porto versus AS Monaco in 2004's "The Rise of the Special One".. 52

The Italian Derby: Juventus vs. AC Milan (2003)........... 57

2005's Liverpool vs. AC Milan matchup: The miraculous Istanbul comeback...60

Chelsea vs. Manchester United in The all English derby (2008).. 64

The Triple Triumph:(2010) Inter Milan vs. Bayern Munich.......... 68

Manchester United vs. Barcelona in 2011, a brilliant display of Barcelona... 71

The Unforgettable 2012 Champions League Journey of Chelsea...75

Bayern Munich and Borussia Dortmund in The Rise of

the Bundesliga (2013)..82

The 2014 "La Decima" Dream match between Real Madrid and
Atletico Madrid..88

Real Madrid versus Atletico Madrid in Ronaldo's
Redemption (2016)..92

Juventus versus Real Madrid on The Cristiano Ronaldo Show in
2017..96

(2018) The Clash of the Titans: Real Madrid vs. Liverpool.
99

Real Madrid's hat-trick of victories under the Zidane era includes
2016, 2017, and 2018..102

The Heroics of Mohamed Salah in the Champions League
in 2019: The Ascension of the Egyptian King.............. 106

A moment in Champions League history................... 111

*The Dutch Maestros: Champions League success for Ajax's Golden
Generation...111

Barcelona's Dominance in the Champions League and
Guardiola's Tiki-Taka Revolution.............................. 116

Barcelona vs. Real Madrid in the Champions League: The Eternal
Rivalry...121

Champions League Highlights: Spectacular Goals and
Dramatic Saves...125

The Champions League's Future...129

Introduction

We cordially invite you to embark on a journey through the illustrious past of the UEFA Champions League, where legends are created, wishes are realized, and immortality is attained.

The Champions League has won the hearts of football fans all across the world *since it began in 1955*. Amazing goals, thrilling comebacks, and astounding talent displays occurred during the tournament, leaving lasting impressions on the history of the beautiful game.

The Champions League has continually given a stage for brilliance, whether it is in historic encounters or outstanding individual performances. A competition that represents the height of quality and triumph in the world of European football captivates the hearts and minds of millions of fans everywhere. The UEFA Champions League, a competition that highlights the best players from the most illustrious clubs on the continent, has produced a great number of memorable moments that will go down in football history. It is an event where legends have risen, dynasties have begun, and records have been broken.

We set out on an exhilarating voyage through time, reliving the key events that have shaped this illustrious competition and solidified its status as the pinnacle of football excellence.

*The origin Champions League's

The most prestigious club football tournament in Europe, *the UEFA Champions League, had its roots in the early 1950s*. The competition has changed names and formats over the years as it has progressed. To bring together the best football clubs from various nations for competitive games, the idea of European club competitions evolved.

The Latin Cup was formed as a match between teams from **France, Spain, Italy, and Portugal in the 1940s**. The Latin Cup served as the prototype for later European club competitions despite its brief existence (**1949–1957**). The success of the Latin Cup sparked interest in a pan-European club competition. **The European Cup was** *first presented by the Union of European Football Associations (UEFA) in 1955*. 16 teams from throughout the continent competed in the inaugural competition, which was held ***during the 1955–1956 season***.

Early European Cup competitions had a direct knockout format, with domestic league champions being allowed to compete. As the competition gained prominence, football fans from all around Europe expressed a lot of interest. Real Madrid emerged as the dominant power, winning the first five championships from ***1956 to 1960*** under the leadership of famous athletes like **Alfredo Di Stefano and Ferenc Puskas**. UEFA attempted to broaden the European Cup to include more teams and increase its popularity as it continued to capture spectators. **The competition was significantly rebranded and given the name "UEFA Champions League" in 1992**.

This modification was made to better represent the competition's pan-European scope and the presence of several league champions. A group stage in addition to the knockout stages was added to the redesigned Champions League. More teams were able to compete because of this structure, which also led to more games being played. There were several groups in the group stage, and clubs competed against one another at home and away. The best teams from each group advanced to the knockout rounds, which culminated in the championship game. The modern period of the Champions League saw growing commercialization, with significant media agreements and sponsorships helping. During this time, there was a change in the balance of power as clubs from other European divisions enjoyed success and displayed a wide range of football skills. The Champions League's format and eligibility requirements have continued to change throughout time. Because more teams are taking part, more clubs from other leagues can now compete. The competition also added a playoff phase to choose the final qualifiers before the group stage. When the *Champions League expanded to include various clubs from the top footballing nations in 1997,* it marked one significant development. Increased representation from nations with a long history of playing football was the goal of this modification. Additionally, the competition continued to improve its qualification process by adding standards based on coefficient rankings and domestic league performance. There have recently been discussions and ideas for additional changes to the Champions League framework. One concept is the creation of a European Super League, in which a small number of elite clubs would compete independently of the current UEFA championships. *But no firm adjustments have been made as of the September 2021* deadline that I am aware of. The Champions League has evolved and has increased in global appeal, making it a recognizable and much-awaited event in the football world.

The Champions League's Unparalleled Drama

Many people consider the UEFA Champions League to be one of the most prestigious and exciting football tournaments in the world. With its gripping matches, surreal comebacks, and flashes of unmatched sports skill, it regularly offers unmatched drama that enthralls viewers. Let's look at a few of the factors that make the Champions League such a dramatic stage.

a contest with high stakes: The Champions League brings together the top clubs from throughout Europe, challenging them to a match for supremacy in the continent. With such elite teams competing, every match becomes a high-stakes contest, and the drama heightens with each subsequent round.

Unpredictability: Unpredictability is a hallmark of the Champions League. No matter how dominating a team may be domestically, they may still have to deal with difficult challenges against opponents they don't frequently play. Dramatic moments arise as a result of underdogs defying the odds and giving outstanding performances.

Forma del knockout: The Champions League's knockout system raises the level of drama to new heights. Teams compete in two-legged matches in the knockout stages, with the outcome decided by the results of the home and away games. As teams compete for vital away goals and the chance to mount thrilling comebacks, this format increases tension and excitement.

Last-minute goal: The Champions League's frequent last-second goals are among its most intriguing features. One team may experience heartache while the other experiences joy as a result of these late strikes, which can dramatically alter the outcome of a game. Such dramatic moments can shape a team's competition experience and leave fans with long-lasting memories.

Comebacks: Over the years, there have been many outstanding comebacks in the Champions League. Against all odds, teams that seemed to be out of the running have come back, creating magnificent drama.

The "Miracle of Istanbul" by Liverpool in 2005 and the "Remontada" by Barcelona against Paris Saint-Germain in 2017 are legendary comebacks that have cemented their places in Champions League lore.

Individual genius: Some of the top players in the world compete in this event, and they frequently have flashes of individual brilliance that can completely change the course of a match. Whether it be a magnificent goal, a fascinating dribble, or a key assist, these individual performances add to the drama and raise the spectacle of the Champions League.

Rivals and storyline lines: Both inside and beyond seasons, the Champions League produces engrossing stories and rivalries. Real Madrid vs. Barcelona, Manchester United vs. Manchester City, and Bayern Munich vs. Borussia Dortmund are just a few examples of fierce rivalries that raise the stakes and fan excitement.

Showdown: The much anticipated Champions League final game, in which the two top clubs compete for the grand prize, serves as the competition's climax. The tournament's culmination, the final showcases the tremendous pressure and ability needed to win the title of European champions and frequently offers spectacular drama.

The unparalleled drama of the Champions League stems from the combination of these factors. It is a league that regularly produces exciting matches, surprising results, and unforgettable moments, enthralling fans around the world and solidifying its position as the summit of club football.

*Real Madrid and AC Milan in the 1958 Clash of the Titans

In 1958, the European Cup final match between Real Madrid and AC Milan was a highly anticipated contest. At the time, both sides were regarded as being titans of European football, therefore the final matchup generated a great deal of interest among football fans. **At the Heysel Stadium in Brussels, Belgium, the game took place on May 28, 1958**. Real Madrid, who had already won the competition the previous two years, was playing in their third straight European Cup final. However, AC Milan was participating in the championship game for the first time. The actual match between these two dominant squads was an exciting one. *Juan Alberto Schiaffino scored the first goal for AC Milan in the second minute to take the lead right away. Alfredo Di Stefano immediately equalized for Real Madrid, though, in the 14th* *minute*. Both teams continued to produce scoring opportunities as the game remained fiercely competitive. With a goal by Francisco Gento in the 60th minute of the second half, Real Madrid was able to take the lead.

AC Milan tried their hardest to equalize, but they were unable. ***Real Madrid maintained their advantage and eventually prevailed 2-1 to win the competition and clinch their third straight European Cup***. The triumph solidified Real Madrid's position as one of the major forces in European football at the time. ***Their main player,***

Alfredo Di Stefano, who was essential to the team's success, also achieved a great deal. When Real Madrid and AC Milan faced off in 1958, it is remembered as a great matchup between two footballing behemoths. It made a significant contribution to the history of European football while showcasing the skill, talent, and tenacity of both teams.

*The impact of the Manchester United crash into the Munich Air Disaster on European

From the devastating Munich Air Disaster to their European victory, Manchester United's journey is a magnificent narrative of resiliency, tenacity, and triumph over adversity. Let's examine the crucial moments that shaped this amazing story. *The Munich Air Disaster happened on February 6, 1958*, when the Manchester United team, known as the "Busby Babes," was on board when the plane crashed in Munich, Germany, as it was taking off. The team had just finished playing Red Star Belgrade in the European Cup. *23 persons were killed in the incident, including numerous club officials and eight Manchester United players*. The catastrophe had a severe effect on Manchester United. *The team lost several of its most promising young players, including Tommy Taylor, Duncan Edwards, and Roger Byrne*. The team needed to be rebuilt, and the club's spirit needed to be revived, according to manager Matt Busby, who suffered terrible injuries in the collision. Against all odds, Busby was able to reassemble the Manchester United team with a combination of graduates from the youth program and fresh additions. The group started to rise from the ashes gradually but surely. They twice made it to the FA Cup final in the years that followed, but they were unable to win the title.

Finally, Manchester United won their first significant prize following the catastrophe in 1963 when they won the FA Cup. This victory represented a turning point and the start of a successful period for the club. *The 1967–68 season was the genuine zenith of Manchester United's comeback. The team started a historic voyage in the European Cup, which is now known as the UEFA Champions League*, under the direction of the famous manager Matt Busby and Bobby Charlton as captain. Manchester United advanced through the tournament's phases by demonstrating their offensive skill and tenacity. *On May 29, 1968, they faced Benfica in the final game at Wembley Stadium in London*. The final turned out to be an exciting contest.

Early on, Benfica had the advantage, but Manchester United's determination and never-say-die spirit won out. Importantly tying the score, *Bobby Charlton's goal forced extra time*. Manchester United showcased their domination in the extra 30 minutes. George Best and Brian Kidd scored goals to secure a 4-1 victory, while Charlton also scored. *After the horror of the Munich Air Disaster, Manchester United made a spectacular return with the victory, which was the first time an English club had ever won the European Cup.*

In addition to bringing the club joy, the European victory served as a metaphor for resiliency and hope. Manchester United had triumphed on the European stage after emerging from the gloom of the Munich Air Disaster. Manchester United became one of the most recognizable and successful clubs in football history as a result of the team's success, which opened doors for later generations. *The Munich Air Disaster is still vividly remembered and plays a crucial role in Manchester United's past*. To ensure that the victims' and survivors' legacies are never forgotten, the club holds an annual remembrance service in their honor. The progression from gloom to brightness is evidence of Manchester United's unbreakable spirit as well as the strength of cohesion and resolve in conquering hardship.

*A memorable upset occurred in 1979 between Nottingham Forest and Malmo FF.

The 1979 European Cup final between Nottingham Forest and Malmö FF is regarded as one of the most spectacular upsets in football history. The renowned Brian Clough-led Nottingham Forest, an English team, defeated Malmö FF, a Swedish team, to win their first European Cup. Nottingham Forest was not then regarded as one of Europe's elite sports teams. They finished in the middle of the pack in their first season back in the First Division after just two years of promotion to the English top division. Nevertheless, they enjoyed a spectacular run in the European Cup, defeating some elite teams en route to the championship game. *At the Olympiastadion in Munich, Germany, on May 30, 1979,* the championship match was held. The Bob Houghton-coached Malmö FF was competing in their first European Cup final. They were regarded as the favorites because of their winning tournament achievements. Malmö FF controlled possession early on and had a few opportunities, but Nottingham Forest eventually took the lead in the 21st minute. The English forward Trevor Francis scored with a diving header to give Forest a 1-0 lead. Malmö FF attempted to cut down Nottingham Forest's lead, but Nottingham Forest managed to maintain it at the break. Malmö FF's offensive attempts were thwarted by Nottingham Forest's steadfast defense in the second half. Malmö had several chances to tie the score but was unable to put the ball in the back of the net. Peter Shilton, the goalkeeper for Nottingham Forest, made many significant stops to preserve his team's advantage. A historic 1-0 upset victory for Nottingham Forest was achieved as the final whistle blew. Since Manchester United's victory in the 1968 European Cup, they became the first English club to do so. As they went on to win the European Cup once more the following year, in 1980, this victory marked the start of Nottingham Forest's most prosperous phase.

The 1979 Nottingham Forest vs. Malmö FF championship game is frequently cited as a prime example of an underdog winning against all odds.

It demonstrated the unpredictable nature and enchantment of football, where a relatively unknown side can rise to the situation and excel on the largest platform.

Ajax vs. AC Milan (1995), The Dutch magnificent run

It was between the Dutch club AFC Ajax and the Italian team AC Milan. *On May 24, 1995, the championship game was held at Vienna, Austria's Ernst Happel Stadium.* Louis van Gaal's Ajax team enjoyed a strong run in the competition before the championship game. *Players like Edwin van der Sar, Frank Rijkaard, Clarence Seedorf, Edgar Davids, and Patrick Kluivert* were on their youthful and promising team. Contrarily, *AC Milan, led by Fabio Capello, boasted veteran players like Franco Baresi, Paolo Maldini, Dejan Savievi, and Marco van Basten*. The contest turned out to be an exciting contest. *Daniele Massaro scored first to give Milan the advantage in the eighth minute*. Ajax, though, reacted quickly and dominated the match with their offensive style of play. *Frank Rijkaard's goal from a corner kick gave Ajax the equalizer in the 12th minute*.

Ajax maintained their offensive brilliance in the second half, and they eventually scored the game-winning goal in the 85th minute. *Ajax took a 2-1 lead thanks to a remarkable goal from Patrick Kluivert,* who was just 18 years old at the time. Ajax hung on to win despite Milan's best efforts to attempt a comeback. This victory was Ajax's fourth European Cup/Champions League championship overall. *It was especially noteworthy because the club had previously won the contest in 1971, 1972, and 1973,* but there had been a protracted gap since then. The triumph also served as a testament to the club's dedication to developing young players and playing entertaining football. One of the most thrilling and unforgettable finals in the history of the league, especially for Ajax supporters, was the 1995 UEFA Champions League final between Ajax and AC Milan.

Juventus vs. Real Madrid (1998): Zidane's Magnificence

Zinedine Zidane's outstanding performance in the 1998 Juventus vs. Real Madrid match is well-remembered. Zidane, who was representing Juventus at the time, put on a masterful display that highlighted his tremendous talent and football savvy. *The game took place in Amsterdam, Netherlands, on May 20, 1998, at the Amsterdam Arena.* One of the most famous club contests in European football was taking place; it was the UEFA Champions League final. After having strong tournaments, *Real Madrid and Juventus both made it to the championship game*. Zidane put on a stunning exhibition of talent, vision, and poise throughout the game, solidifying his position as one of the top midfielders in the world. *With his accurate passing, superb ball control, and extraordinary ability to control the game's speed, he effectively commanded the midfield*. The first goal of the game was assisted by the French playmaker. **He sent an expertly timed ball to Alessandro Del Piero in the 66th minute, and Del Piero scored to give Juventus the lead**. That aim was greatly aided by Zidane's vision and strategy. Juventus and Zidane suffered a painful loss; they had intended to win the famous title. But Zidane's performance in that game cemented his status as one of the finest midfielders of his generation.

Fans and analysts alike were profoundly affected by his ability to exert control over the game, *generate opportunities, and demonstrate amazing talent with the ball.* **Zinedine Zidane** went on to have a very successful career and garnered many honors and titles. ***The Juventus vs. Real Madrid game in 1998 demonstrated Zidane's brilliance and his ability to influence the game with his exceptional skills and football intelligence.*** He later joined Real Madrid as a player in 2001 and later returned to the club as a manager, leading them to three consecutive UEFA Champions League titles from 2016 to 2018. It's still one of his most notable performances throughout his storied career.

Manchester United's Late Heroes: The 1999 Matchup with Bayern Munich

Many people consider the 1999 UEFA Champions League final between Manchester United and Bayern Munich to be one of the sport's most thrilling contests. *On May 26, 1999, it happened in the Camp Nou stadium in Barcelona, Spain.* For the most part, *Bayern Munich controlled the game, and they took the lead in the sixth minute*. Bayern managed to hold onto their lead the entire game thanks to strong defending and controlled play after Mario Basler struck a free kick from the edge of the area. Manchester United appeared to be losing its chance to win the Champions League as the game came to a close. The game, however, changed dramatically in the closing minutes. *Ole Gunnar Solskjaer and Teddy Sheringham were inserted into the game in the 90th minute by Manchester United manager Sir Alex Ferguson. Sheringham was able to score a goal for Manchester United in the first minute of extra time (90+1).* Ryan Giggs' corner kick was flicked on by Sheringham, who then slammed the ball into the goal, throwing the United supporters into a frenzy. However, Manchester United wasn't done yet. The game appeared set for extra time. Just before the final horn sounded, *in the 93rd minute (90+3),* United was given another corner kick. Sheringham once again had a significant impact as David Beckham won it this time.

He directed the ball in the direction of Solskjaer, who used his right foot to deflect it into the goal. The thrilling, late goals changed the course of the match and gave Manchester United an unprecedented treble.

They had already won the FA Cup and the Premier League earlier in the season, and now they had finished the set by taking home the UEFA Champions League.

Manchester United's never-say-die attitude and the influence of their substitutions were on display in the game, which will be remembered for both. *As the first British manager to win the Champions League since its renaming in 1992, it was also a notable accomplishment for Sir Alex Ferguson*.

One of the most famous moments in the club's history is the 1999 Champions League final between Manchester United and Bayern Munich, which is frequently referred to as the "Treble Triumph.

Valencia vs. Real Madrid in The Spanish Showdown (2000)

Football fans eagerly anticipated the Spanish Showdown between Real Madrid and Valencia in the year 2000. In Spanish football, both teams were dominant forces, and they were bitter rivals.

The **game was played on May 24, 2000, at Paris, France's Stade de France**. The UEFA Champions League final, the most esteemed club championship in European football, was taking place. Following successful tournament runs, **Real Madrid and Valencia both made it to the championship game. After extra time, the score remained tied at 1-1, forcing a penalty shootout to decide the winner**. Real Madrid's Fernando Morientes scored the game's first goal in the 39th minute, but Gaizka Mendieta of Valencia tied it up in the first minute of first-half injury time by converting a penalty. It was a stressful situation as each team took turns converting their spot-kicks in the penalty shootout. ***Ultimately, Real Madrid won the shootout 3-0 to claim victory***. Iker Casillas, their goalkeeper, played a critical part in preserving the victory for his club by stopping three penalty kicks. Real Madrid became one of the most successful clubs in the history of the competition with this victory, ***which was their seventh European Cup/Champions League triumph***. Valencia, on the other side, went through heartache after making it to the final for the first time in their history but failing to win the championship. The 2000 Spanish Showdown between Real Madrid and Valencia, which demonstrated the drama and excitement that can develop in a high-stakes final, is still seen as a pivotal moment in football history.

Real Madrid vs. Bayer Leverkusen (2002): Zinedine Zidane's Glorious Moment

Many people consider Zinedine Zidane's stroke of genius during the 2002 UEFA Champions League final between Real Madrid and Bayer Leverkusen to be one of the best goals in the competition's history. *The game was played on May 15, 2002, at Glasgow, Scotland's Hampden Park.* The most important trophy in club football in Europe was up for grabs between *Real Madrid and Bayer Leverkusen. With the score locked at 1-1 in the 45th minute of the* game, Zidane delivered a stroke of pure genius. From the left side, Roberto

Carlos fired a high cross into the box that appeared to be leaving the field of play. *Zidane, though, positioned himself properly and produced an incredible volley with his left foot, which is his weaker foot*.

The ball was struck with power and accuracy by the French maestro, who made a lovely connection with it. *Hans-Jorg Butt*, the defenseless goalkeeper for Bayer Leverkusen, was unable to stop the ball from crashing into the top corner of the goal. It was a stunning demonstration of skill, poise, and audacity. *Zidane's goal ended up being the game-winning score as Real Madrid hung on to win 2-1 and win their eighth European Cup/Champions League championship.*

The shot is frequently called "*The Goal of the Century*" or just "*Zidane's Volley*. Zidane's brilliant performance in the 2002 Champions League final solidified his place among the sport's all-time greats. He became a football superstar due to his talent, grace, and capacity to create magic on the grandest platforms. The goal is still imprinted in the minds of football fans all across the world as a lasting reminder of his extraordinary talent.

Porto versus AS Monaco in 2004's "The Rise of the Special One"

For José Mourinho, who was the manager of Porto at the time, the 2004 UEFA Champions League final between Porto and AS Monaco is frequently regarded as a defining moment. It was a crucial game that demonstrated Mourinho's mastery of strategy and his capacity to lead an underdog club to victory. *On May 26, 2004, the championship match was held in the Arena Auf Schalke in Gelsenkirchen, Germany*. Due to their victories over more prestigious and favored rivals along the way, both clubs' appearances in the championship game shocked many people by surprise. Throughout the competition, José Mourinho's Porto team excelled with their controlled and disciplined play. On the other hand, Didier Deschamps' AS Monaco team, which featured players *like Ludovic*

Giuly and Fernando Morientes, attracted a lot of attention with their youthful and talented roster. *In the 39th minute of the game, Porto took the lead for the first time thanks to a powerful drive from Carlos Alberto that found the bottom corner of the net to give his club a 1-0 lead*.

The goal demonstrated Porto's attacking potential and their capacity to find openings in the defense of their opponents. Monaco attempted to build a comeback in the second half, but their attempts were denied by Porto's strong defense, which Mourinho had skillfully put together. Monaco attempted to assault, but Porto remained unwavering, preventing any clear-cut opportunities for their adversaries. ***Deco, one of the standout performers of the competition, scored a fantastic goal to make it 2-0 in the 71st minute to give Porto the victory.*** Deco received the ball outside the box, then unleashed a shot that curled into the top corner and gave the Monaco goalie no chance. Porto maintained their lead until the final horn, and AS Monaco found it difficult to get back into the game.

Porto's 2-0 victory gave them their second-ever European championship and the UEFA Champions League trophy, The victory represented a significant step forward for Mourinho, who had up to that moment been mostly unknown on the international stage. Throughout the competition, but notably in the championship game, his tactical prowess and capacity to bring out the best in his players were on full display. Mourinho's accomplishments at Porto opened the door for his ascent to notoriety in the world of football administration. He continued to be successful and gained a reputation as one of the most successful and significant coaches in contemporary football while managing several elite clubs, *including Chelsea, Inter Milan, Real Madrid, and Manchester United.*

The Italian Derby: Juventus vs. AC Milan (2003)

The Italian derby alludes to a well-known soccer game between AC

Milan and Juventus that happened on **May 28, 2003.** It was the UEFA Champions League final, taking place at Old Trafford in Manchester, England. Because it involved two of the most renowned and successful football clubs in Italy, the game was eagerly awaited. **With players like Paolo Maldini, Andrea Pirlo, Clarence Seedorf, and Filippo Inzaghi** on the roster, AC Milan had a potent squad under the direction of manager Carlo Ancelotti. **Alessandro Del Piero, Pavel Nedved, and Gianluigi Buffon** were among the talents on Juventus' star-studded roster, which was coached by Marcello Lippi.

After extra time, the game, which was hotly contested, concluded with a score of 0-0. The outcome of the game was then decided by a penalty shootout. ***After a 3-2 victory on penalties, AC Milan was declared the winner.*** Dida, the goalie for AC Milan, saved critical shots during the penalty shootout to win the game. Milan won the sixth European Cup/Champions League title in club history after Andriy Shevchenko converted the game-winning penalty.

A dramatic and highly contested match between two of Italy's football heavies, the 2003 Champions League final is frequently recalled. With their triumph in the penalty shootout, AC Milan cemented their place in football history and their position as one of the premier clubs in Europe.

2005's Liverpool vs. AC Milan matchup: The miraculous Istanbul comeback

The UEFA Champions League Final between **Liverpool FC and AC Milan,**

which took place on May 25, 2005, at the ***Atatürk Olympic Stadium in Istanbul, Turkey***, is referred to as "The Miracle of Istanbul." One of the greatest comebacks in football history, in the opinion of many. AC Milan dominated the first half of the game and jumped out to a commanding *3-0 lead thanks to Paolo Maldini and a brace from Hernan Crespo*. The Italian club was unstoppable and looked like it was about to win its ninth Champions League title. However, the second half of the game brought about an unexpected change. Liverpool's stunning comeback will live on in football lore forever. *Steven Gerrard scored to start the comeback in the 54th minute,* and *Vladimir Smicer added another goal two minutes later. Liverpool continued to play when the score was 3-2* to tie the game. In the 60th minute, Dida of Milan saved *Xabi Alonso's penalty attempt, but Alonso was quick to capitalize on the rebound and* square the score *at 3-3. Since neither team was able to score the game-winning goal in extra time, a penalty shootout was necessary.*

The Liverpool goalie, Jerzy Dudek, was the shootout's unsung hero thanks to two crucial stops and an unusual dancing-like skill on the goal line. *Liverpool eventually won the game and the European Cup/Champions League 3-2 on penalties.*

The victory was nothing short of amazing given the unlikely odds they faced at the halfway mark. Due to Liverpool's amazing recovery and their ability to overcome a three-goal deficit against a strong AC Milan club, the match is frequently referred to as the Miracle of Istanbul. It continues to be regarded as one of the most famous moments in UEFA Champions League history by Liverpool supporters all around the world.

Chelsea vs. Manchester United in The all English derby (2008)

Moscow's "The Thriller." *The match between Manchester United and Chelsea, which took place on May 21, 2008, at the Luzhniki Stadium in Moscow, Russia,* was exhilarating and historic. The UEFA Champions League, the most important trophy in European club football, was at stake in this match between two English clubs, therefore it was eagerly awaited. Both Avram Grant of Chelsea and Sir Alex Ferguson of Manchester United were vying for the coveted championship.

A dramatic penalty shootout ensued after the game ended in a 1-1 draw after extra time. In the 26th minute,

Cristiano Ronaldo headed home a cross from Wes Brown to give Manchester United the lead. But in the 45th minute, *Frank Lampard scored Chelsea's equalizer after pouncing on a stray ball inside the box.* In the remaining minutes of play, both teams had numerous scoring chances, but neither was able to score the game-winning goal. Extra time was played in the **game, but there were no goals scored during it, so the score remained locked at 1-1 when the final horn sounded**. After that, a penalty shootout was used to settle the game. **Ronaldo missed Manchester United's third penalty**, *although the first seven penalties were all successfully converted.* **John Terry, the captain of Chelsea, had a chance to win it for his club but slipped while attempting to take a penalty and hit the post**. Edwin van der Sar, the goalie for Manchester United, stopped Nicolas Anelka's penalty in sudden death to give **Manchester United a 6-5 shootout** *victory. **Manchester United won the UEFA Champions League for the third time with this victory, joining their victories in 1968 and 1999**.* The victory brought an unforgettable season to a close for Manchester United, who also won the Premier League title, completing a domestic and European double. The 2008 Champions League Final is remembered as one of the most dramatic games in modern football history, largely because of how intense the penalty shootout was.

The Triple Triumph:(2010) Inter Milan vs. Bayern Munich

Inter Milan's 2009–2010 treble victory was a rare feat in football history. By winning three significant trophies-the ***Serie A championship, the Coppa Italia, and the UEFA Champions League-Inter Milan, led by José***

Mourinho, attained an extraordinary degree of achievement. Bayern Munich and Inter Milan, *however, faced off in that year's Champions League final. At the Santiago Bernabeu Stadium in Madrid, Spain, on May 22, 2010*, the championship game was held. The contest between these two strong European clubs was heated and eagerly anticipated. Mourinho's Inter Milan employed a strong defensive strategy, whilst Louis van Gaal's Bayern Munich team excelled at attacking. *When Diego Milito successfully beat Bayern Munich goalkeeper Hans-Jorg Butt with a well-placed effort in the*

35th minute, Inter Milan seized the lead. *Milito, who increased Inter's lead in the 70th minute with another precise strike, emerged as the game's hero*. A dramatic conclusion was set up when *Bayern Munich battled back and scored one goal through Thomas Muller in the 80th minute*. But Inter Milan defended staunchly until the last siren, maintaining their advantage. Inter Milan won this match, completing the treble, and became the first Italian club to do so. *After winning it with Porto in 2004, José Mourinho became just the third manager in history to win the Champions League with two* *different clubs*. Inter Milan's 2010 treble victory established them as one of the most successful teams in European football and represented a crucial turning point in the club's history. The squad's ability to take home three major medals in a single campaign demonstrated its fortitude, focus, and tactical skill. The highlight of their illustrious year was their triumph in the Champions League final over Bayern Munich.

Manchester United vs. Barcelona in 2011, a brilliant display of Barcelona

Taking place **on May 28, 2011**, at **Wembley Stadium in London, England,** was the UEFA Champions League final between Manchester United and Barcelona. The game is frequently cited as one of Barcelona's most resounding victories and is regarded as a demonstration of their greatness at the time. **With a 3-1 victory against the opposition, Barcelona won the game and the Champions League**, giving them their fourth overall championship. **Barcelona was the first team to win the trophy three times in the last six years, making this victory more noteworthy for them**. Being two of the most successful and well-liked teams in Europe at the time, Manchester United and Barcelona added to the excitement surrounding the match. *Quick, short passes and a possession-based game were hallmarks of Barcelona's "tiki-taka" style of play,* which was well-liked by football fans. *Pedro Rodriguez of Barcelona scored the game's first goal in the 27th minute after a fantastic team effort*. The English team gained hope when *Wayne Rooney of Manchester United equalized with a skillfully scored goal in the 34th minute*. But Barcelona ultimately proved to be the superior team, as they took the lead again right before the break. Barcelona's star player, Lionel *Messi, demonstrated his talent by netting a spectacular goal in the 54th minute*, demonstrating his amazing dribbling skills and finishing ability. *In the 69th minute, Barcelona's*

David Villa put the game out of reach with a beautiful curling shot. Barcelona's superior performance and overall control of the game proved to be too much for Manchester United to handle, despite their best efforts to stage a comeback. Barcelona's deft passing and individual skill were on full show in the game, which was praised as a masterclass in football. The 2011 UEFA Champions League final between Barcelona and Manchester United showcased Barcelona's brilliance and their ability to play mesmerizing football, leaving a lasting impression on football fans worldwide.

It reaffirmed Barcelona's status as one of the greatest teams of that era and emphasized their dominance in European football during that time.

The Unforgettable 2012 Champions League Journey of Chelsea

Chelsea Football Club entered the 2011–2012 UEFA Champions League and began an extraordinary journey that earned them the moniker "Comeback Kings."

The team's outstanding performance and ultimate victory in the championship game will always be remembered in the annals of the event. *The Chelsea team was placed in Group E with Valencia, Bayer Leverkusen, and Genk at the start of the group stage.* The Blues had a strong season, finishing first in their division with four victories, one draw, and one defeat. *They totaled 13 goals while only giving up three.* Chelsea, who had advanced to the knockout rounds, played Italian team Napoli in the Round of 16.

The Blues lost 3-1 in the first leg, which was contested at the Stadio San Paolo in Napoli. When they returned to Stamford Bridge for the second leg, the odds were stacked against them. *With goals from Didier Drogba, John Terry, Frank Lampard, and Branislav Ivanovic, Chelsea made an amazing comeback to win the game 4-1 in overtime*. Chelsea advanced to the quarterfinals with a 5-4 overall score, *Chelsea met the champions of*

Portugal, Benfica, in the quarterfinals. Salomon Kalou's injury-time goal gave the Blues a 1-0 win in the first leg, which was contested at Benfica's Estadio da Luz. *Frank Lampard and Raul Meireles scored for Chelsea in the second leg at Stamford Bridge to secure a 2-1 triumph. They qualified for the semifinals with a 3-1 overall score.* The defending champions, Barcelona, and their all-star striker Lionel Messi were matched up against Chelsea in the semi-final draw. Didier Drogba gave Chelsea the lead at Stamford Bridge in the first leg with a goal, but Lionel Messi's penalty kick conversion gave Barcelona the tie. However, the first-half red card for Chelsea's captain, John Terry, turned the game around. *The Blues fought courageously in defense despite being down to ten men, and the match concluded in a draw at 1-1*. One of the most thrilling games in Champions League history was the second leg, which took place at Camp Nou in Barcelona. Sergio Busquets gave Barcelona the lead, but Ramires gave Chelsea the lead shortly before halftime with an incredible goal. *Barcelona continued to press forward after the final score was knotted at 2-2 on a combined basis*, but Chelsea's defense stood firm thanks to the valiant efforts of players like Gary Cahill and Ashley Cole. *Chelsea earned a 2-2 draw on the night and a 3-2 triumph overall thanks to a counterattack by Fernando Torres in the waning moments of the game*. Torres calmly slipped the ball past the Barcelona goalie. *The Blues had advanced to their second Champions League final in club history. Chelsea met Bayern Munich*, the tournament favorites playing on their home field, in the championship match, which was played at the Allianz Arena in Munich, Germany. *Thomas*

Müller's goal for Bayern gave them the lead in the 83rd minute. But once more, Chelsea's tenacity was on display as *Didier Drogba scored a dramatic equalizer in the 88th minute to force extra time. Bayern applied consistent pressure, but the score stayed tied, forcing a penalty shootout.* Chelsea maintained composure during the stressful penalty shootout. *Didier Drogba stepped up to the spot and converted the game-winning penalty to give Chelsea a 4-3 victory with the scores tied at 3-3. For the first time in their history,* the Blues were named European champions, and their comeback trip ended with a win that will live in infamy.

The outstanding performance of Chelsea in the 2011–2012 UEFA Champions League demonstrated their tenacity, tenacity, and capacity to overcome obstacles. Their ability to come back from seemingly impossible situations earned them the moniker of "Comeback Kings" and left an indelible mark on the competition's history.

Bayern Munich and Borussia Dortmund in The Rise of the Bundesliga (2013)

Over the years, the rivalry between Bayern Munich and Borussia Dortmund has been one of the most heated and exciting games in German football. In particular, *the 2013 campaign demonstrated the intense rivalry*

between these two clubs and contributed to the rise of the Bundesliga. Bayern Munich was determined to recover their place as the dominant force in German football in the 2012–2013 season, led by their newly appointed manager Jupp Heynckes.

However, *Borussia Dortmund, under the charismatic leadership of Jürgen Klopp, was aiming to defend their back-to-back Bundesliga titles and solidify their position as a true superpower*. Both clubs played outstanding football all season long, delighting both the crowd and the observers. Bayern Munich, with their all-star team, demonstrated their strength and dependability by winning every game. Borussia Dortmund, renowned for their brisk attacking style and young, skilled players, presented tough competition and worked hard to defend their crown.

The UEFA Champions League final, which pitted Bayern Munich against Borussia Dortmund at Wembley Stadium in London on May 25, 2013, served as the season's high point. A titanic match between two German clubs was ready to take place, displaying the Bundesliga's growing might and caliber on the European scene. *Bayern Munich defeated Borussia Dortmund 2-1 in a hotly contested encounter that was* widely anticipated. *Mario Mandzukic, a striker from Croatia, gave Bayern Munich the lead in the 60th minute*, but *Ilkay Gündogan, a player from Dortmund, equalized* from the penalty spot. *Arjen Robben, a Dutch winger for Bayern Munich, emerged as the game's unsung hero with the score tied as it entered the final moments*. Bayern Munich won the Champions League championship after Robben capitalized on an opportunity in the 89th minute to score the game-winning goal. Bayern Munich's victory in the Champions League final was a turning moment in their career and heralded both a domestic and a renaissance in Europe. *In addition to winning the DFB-Pokal (German Cup), they went on to win the Bundesliga that season, completing a remarkable treble. Bayern Munich's domination during the 2012–2013 campaign demonstrated their capacity to retake the title of the top German football club.*

While Borussia Dortmund fell short in the Champions League final, their performance throughout the season was commendable. As runners-up in the Bundesliga, they continued to astonish soccer fans across the world with their offensive style of play. A pivotal period in the development of the Bundesliga was the 2013 season between Bayern Munich and Borussia Dortmund. It demonstrated the depth and caliber of German football and laid the foundation for a long-lasting rivalry between these two clubs in the years to come.

The 2014 "La Decima" Dream match between Real Madrid and Atletico Madrid

It's common to refer to the 2014 UEFA Champions League final between Real Madrid and Atletico Madrid as a "La Decima" dream game. *The Estádio da Luz in Lisbon, Portugal, hosted a highly*

anticipated and historic match on May 24, 2014. Real Madrid, one of the best football teams in the world, has been without a European Cup or Champions League championship for 12 years. *Their local rivals, Atletico Madrid*, were attempting to win their first-ever Champions League championship and cap off an outstanding campaign under manager Diego Simeone.

Atletico Madrid scored the game's first goal in the 36th minute on an assist from Diego Godin. They maintained their lead for the majority of the game by resolutely defending and hindering Real Madrid's offensive attempts.

Sergio Ramos of Real Madrid scored a thrilling equalizer in the 93rd minute, forcing extra time. Real Madrid's superior fitness and depth started to emerge during the extra time. *Real Madrid won 4-1 thanks to goals from Cristiano Ronaldo, Marcelo, and Gareth Bale in the 110th, 118th, and*

120th minutes, respectively. *The goals by Bale and Ronaldo stood out in particular*; Bale's shot was a spectacular overhead kick, and Ronaldo's goal gave Real Madrid the victory. *The title "La Decima" refers to Real Madrid's 10th European Cup/Champions League victory*. They became the *first team to win ten European Cups*, making it a historic accomplishment for the club and their supporters. In contrast, Atletico Madrid's hopes of capturing their first Champions League championship were dashed, but they were praised for their outstanding play throughout the competition.

Under Simeone's direction, they demonstrated defensive sturdiness and tenacity during their run to the final. **Real Madrid's victory in the 2014 UEFA Champions League final against Atletico Madrid, which gave them their long-awaited 10th European Cup/Champions League trophy,** will always be remembered as an exciting and dramatic game.

Real Madrid versus Atletico Madrid in Ronaldo's Redemption (2016)

In the UEFA Champions League final, there was a fierce and eagerly anticipated confrontation between two rival clubs. *The San Siro Stadium in Milan, Italy, hosted it on May 28, 2016*. For *Cristiano Ronaldo, this game is*

important because it gave him a second chance to prove himself after a bad performance in a previous Champions League final.

Despite Ronaldo's best efforts, he didn't have a particularly exciting game against Atletico Madrid in the 2014 final. Ronaldo failed to have a meaningful impact on the scoreboard as Real Madrid ultimately prevailed 4-1 after extra time. *In 2016, Ronaldo was motivated to make amends and once more demonstrate his prowess on the largest platform.*

Ronaldo performed admirably in the 2016 final, which featured a rematch between the two Madrid clubs. Both teams demonstrated their defensive strength during the closely contested game. The game went into overtime after regulation ended in a scoreless draw. Ronaldo had his first impact in the 98th minute. With a strong header from a cross that Gareth Bale supplied, he gave Real Madrid the lead. Real Madrid now had the advantage, and the tide had turned in their favor. ***Real Madrid defeated their opponents 3-0 as a result of goals from Ronaldo and*** *several of his teammates, including Gareth Bale.*

This triumph was Real Madrid's second in three years and their eleventh European Cup/Champions League triumph overall. The triumph was made possible in large part by Ronaldo's goal, which also brought about the atonement he so desperately needed. Ronaldo's fortitude and capacity to execute under duress were on display in the 2016 Champions League final. It confirmed his position as one of the best players of his time and illustrated his influence on football's grandest stage.

Juventus versus Real Madrid on The Cristiano Ronaldo Show in 2017

The 2017 UEFA Champions League battle between Juventus and Real Madrid, dubbed *"The Cristiano Ronaldo Show," was eagerly anticipated.* During the 2016–2017 Champions League season, *Juventus, an Italian club, and Real Madrid, a Spanish club, played each other in a quarterfinal match*. The match's second leg was played at the Santiago

Bernabeu Stadium in Madrid, Spain, on *April 11, 2017*, after the first leg was held *on April 3 at the Juventus Stadium in Turin, Italy*. Juventus displayed a great defensive effort in the first leg and was able to contain Real Madrid's onslaught. *Cristiano Ronaldo scored an important away goal for Real Madrid*, and *Paulo Dybala netted for Juventus as the game concluded in a 1-1 tie*. At the Santiago Bernabeu Stadium, Cristiano Ronaldo's exceptional talent and skills were on display during the second leg. The game was dominated by Real Madrid from the outset. *Ronaldo scored the game's first goal* past Juventus goalkeeper Gianluigi Buffon in the third minute.

In the 64th and 90th minutes, he scored two more goals to complete his hat-trick. Real Madrid also received a goal from Marco Asensio, giving the hosts a 4-1 triumph.

Particularly impressive was Cristiano Ronaldo's hat trick in the second leg, which demonstrated his propensity for giving his best in big games. Ronaldo's brilliance contributed significantly to Real Madrid defeating Juventus 6-3 on the road and moving them into the Champions League semi-finals.

Real Madrid's victory and Cristiano Ronaldo's key performance throughout the competition cemented his place as one of the all-time great footballers.

(2018) The Clash of the Titans: Real Madrid vs. Liverpool

on *May 26, 2018*, in *Kyiv, Ukraine*, at the *NSC Olimpiyskiy Stadium during the UEFA Champions League final*. It was a highly anticipated game between two of the biggest football clubs in Europe. *Real Madrid prevailed, defeating Liverpool 3-1 to win the Champions League for a record third time in a row*. Karim Benzema and Gareth Bale scored goals for Real Madrid, while Sadio Mane scored the lone goal for Liverpool. *The match's crucial turning moment occurred when Mohamed Salah, the top player for Liverpool, was forced off the field in the 30th minute after suffering a shoulder injury during a collision with Sergio Ramos of Real Madrid*. The loss of Salah significantly impacted Liverpool's ability to attack. Following Salah's injury, Real Madrid's Karim Benzema scored the game's first goal in the 51st minute by capitalizing on a Loris Karius error for Liverpool. A few minutes later, Sadio Mane restored Liverpool's lead, but Gareth Bale scored two goals for Real Madrid after coming off the bench. His second goal, a spectacular overhead kick, stands out in particular.

Real Madrid won their fourth Champions League championship in the past five years, giving them their 13th overall and fourth under manager Zinedine Zidane. The 2018 Champions League final between Liverpool and Real Madrid was a highly anticipated and thrilling game that displayed the quality and excitement of European football at the top level. It was a heartbreaking outcome for Liverpool, who had a wonderful campaign but fell short in the final.

Real Madrid's hat-trick of victories under the Zidane era includes 2016, 2017, and 2018.

The time when renowned French footballer Zinedine Zidane managed Real Madrid, from 2016 to 2018, is referred to as the "Zidane Era." Real Madrid won the renowned competition three times in a row during this time, completing an incredible hat-trick of triumphs in the UEFA Champions League.

The UEFA Champions League for 2016: Real Madrid face Atletico Madrid in the UEFA Champions League championship game during Zidane's first season as manager. On May 28, 2016, the game was played at Milan's San Siro stadium.

The game went into overtime after regulation ended in a 0-0 draw. **With a 5-3 victory on penalties**, Real Madrid was declared the winner. Real Madrid won their 11th Champions League championship with this triumph.

The UEFA Champions League for 2017: The following year in the Champions League, Real Madrid continued to have success.

At Cardiff's Principality Stadium on June 3, 2017, they played Juventus in the championship match. With a score of 4-1, ***Real Madrid easily prevailed in the game. Casemiro and Marco Asensio*** *also scored goals, and Cristiano Ronaldo played a key role with a brace*. With this triumph, Real Madrid won their 12th Champions League championship.

The UEFA Champions League for 2018: As the first team to accomplish such a feat in the tournament's contemporary period, Real Madrid made history by winning the Champions League for a third straight year. At the NSC Olimpiyskiy Stadium in Kyiv, Ukraine, on May 26, 2018, Real Madrid and Liverpool squared off in the championship game. ***Karim Benzema***

and a magnificent overhead kick by Gareth Bale gave them a 3-1 victory. It was Real Madrid's 13th Champions League triumph with this victory. Real Madrid's supremacy in European competition, which demonstrated their capacity to consistently play at the greatest level, served as a defining feature of the Zidane era. Real Madrid's success during this time was largely due to Zidane's tactical nous, his formidable man-management abilities, and the outstanding performances of important players like Cristiano Ronaldo.

The Heroics of Mohamed Salah in the Champions League in 2019: The Ascension of the Egyptian King

The heroics of Mohamed Salah in the 2019 UEFA Champions League stood out and drew the attention of football fans all around the world. *The "Egyptian King," Salah, was*

instrumental in Liverpool FC's historic journey to the Champions League final that year. In the 2017–18 season, Salah's first with Liverpool, he had already established himself as one of the most productive forwards in European football. He was a fearsome force in the Premier League thanks to his pace, talent, and precise finishing ability. Salah, however, really shone in the Champions League. Salah had a crucial role in many of the dramatic situations that occurred during Liverpool's 2019 run to the final. He helped Liverpool advance to the knockout stages during the group stage by scoring important goals against *Paris Saint-Germain, Red Star Belgrade, and Napoli.* Salah was crucial to Liverpool's victory against Porto in the quarterfinals.

He helped Liverpool secure a decisive 6-1 aggregate victory with a spectacular long-range goal in the first game and an assist in the second. Salah's exploits stood out during the semifinal matchup with Barcelona. Liverpool's chances of moving on appeared limited after losing the first leg 3-0 at Camp Nou. ***Salah stepped up and led the comeback during the second leg at***

Anfield. Salah scored the game's first goal with a perfectly placed finish in the 34th minute, giving Liverpool new hope. A spectacular 4-0 victory over Barcelona was completed by Divock Origi, who scored twice in the second half, including a late winner to advance Liverpool to the championship game. *Salah was present again in the final game against Tottenham Hotspur.* While he didn't score in this particular game, his influence on the outcome was apparent. He earned a penalty in the first minute, which teammate Divock Origi converted to give Liverpool a 2-0 victory and their sixth Champions League crown.

Throughout the entire 2019 Champions League season, Salah showed off his tremendous skill, calmness, and capacity to perform in pressure-filled situations. His achievements not only cemented his place among the top players in the world but also made him a legend among Liverpool supporters. Salah's heroics in the Champions League that year highlighted his value to the team and showed that he was capable of performing under pressure on the highest platform.

His services were crucial to Liverpool's victory, and he appropriately received considerable acclaim for his competition performances.

A moment in Champions League history

*The Dutch Maestros: Champions League success for Ajax's Golden Generation

The term *"Ajax's Golden Generation" refers to a time in the early 1970s when AFC Ajax, one of the most prosperous football clubs in the Netherlands*, enjoyed outstanding success in the European Cup, which is now known as the UEFA Champions League. Ajax, **under the guidance of Rinus Michels** and captained by **Johan Cruyff**, transformed the sport with their ground-breaking brand of "Total Football.

The 1965–1966 season marked the start of Ajax's Golden Generation's journey as they claimed their first Eredivisie championship. This victory signaled the beginning of a period that will rule Dutch and European football. **From 1965 through 1970**, Ajax won six straight Eredivisie championships, which served as a springboard for their success in Europe. Ajax's playing strategy was based on quick transitions between positions, aggressive football, and fluid movement under Rinus Michels' direction. Ajax became a dominant force in European competitions thanks to Total Football's emphasis on adaptability and players' smooth positional switching.

When Ajax won their first European Cup during the 1970–1971 season, the Golden Generation reached its zenith. Dick van Dijk and Arie Haan each scored once as Ajax defeated

Panathinaikos 2-0 in the championship match. Throughout the competition, the club showed off its offensive skill and technical mastery, winning games against Liverpool and Atletico Madrid, two formidable foes. The following years saw more success for Ajax. *They established themselves as one of the best club teams in history by winning three straight European Cups from 1971 to 1973*. With excellent players like *Johan Cruyff, Johan Neeskens, Piet Keizer, Ruud Krol, and many others*, the team won numerous European championships. *The mid-1970s saw the unfortunate end of Ajax's Golden*

Generation as several important players left for other teams. But the legacy of their accomplishments persisted, and future generations of football players and coaches were still influenced by their influence on the tactics and style of the game. It's important to note that Ajax has recently had a comeback in European competitions, even though it might not be considered a new Golden Generation. Under the leadership of Erik ten Hag, the team has seen success in the UEFA Champions League, making it to the semifinals in the 2018–19 campaign. With a young team that had players with talent like Frenkie de Jong and Matthijs de Ligt, they displayed an exciting brand of football and won over fans. Even though they lost the tournament, their performance was praised by football fans all around the world.

Barcelona's Dominance in the Champions League and Guardiola's Tiki-Taka Revolution

The term "Guardiola's Tiki-Taka Revolution" describes the tactical system Pep Guardiola used while *leading FC Barcelona, particularly between 2008 and 2012.*

A possession-based play style known as tiki-taka emphasizes quick, short passes, moving away from the ball, and keeping possession of the ball for longer periods to maintain game control. Barcelona experienced tremendous success under Guardiola's leadership, sweeping both national and international competitions. The team's win in the UEFA Champions League, Europe's top club competition, was its most notable accomplishment during this time. Under Guardiola, *Barcelona won the UEFA Champions League twice, in the 2008–2009 and 2010–2011* campaigns.

The team gave outstanding results in both campaigns, demonstrating their command of the Tiki-Taka design. The club was virtually unstoppable thanks to their proficiency in maintaining possession, executing complicated passing schemes, and finding openings in the defense of their opponents. *Barcelona's 2008–2009 season will always be remembered for their victory over Manchester United in the Rome-based final.* Barcelona won the game 2-0 with two goals from Samuel Eto'o and Lionel Messi. Barcelona won their first Champions League trophy under Guardiola and their third overall with this victory. *Barcelona advanced to the Champions League final in the 2010–2011 campaign when they faced Manchester United at Wembley Stadium.*

Barcelona performed brilliantly, winning the game 3-1. The triumph was sealed by *goals from Pedro, Lionel Messi, and David Villa*, showcasing the team's great attacking skills and capacity to demolish the formidable competition.

The Tiki-Taka Revolution under Guardiola not only resulted in trophy success but also had a long-lasting effect on the game of football. Barcelona's playing style was imitated by several teams and managers, and parts of Tiki-Taka are currently used by numerous clubs and leagues throughout the world. Guardiola's play style at Barcelona altered how football is viewed and enjoyed, making an ever-lasting impact on the game.

Barcelona vs. Real Madrid in the Champions League: The Eternal Rivalry

One of the most passionate and legendary rivalries in football history is that between Barcelona and Real Madrid. The stakes are much higher when these two clubs face off in the UEFA Champions League since they are vying for European supremacy. Let's examine the dynamics of this famous Champions League rivalry. First off, *Real Madrid and Barcelona are two of the Champions League's most illustrious teams*, they have won a total of 17 European Cup/Champions League championships. Real Madrid holds the tournament record with 13 victories, while Barcelona has won the title four times.

Their Champions League matches are frequently eagerly anticipated and draw a large crowd. The contests are characterized by great determination, extraordinary skill, and harsh competition. In addition to showcasing team pride, these matches also serve to highlight the historical and cultural contrasts between Barcelona and Madrid as well as the two cities' respective cities. Star players are present on both teams, further escalating the rivalry. *The Champions League triumphs of Barcelona over the years have been greatly aided by players like Lionel Messi, Xavi Hernandez, Andrés Iniesta, and Carles Puyol.* On the other side, Real Madrid has had legendary players who have had a long-lasting influence on the competition, *including Cristiano Ronaldo, Raul González, Iker Casillas, and Zinedine Zidane.*

In the 2010–2011 season's semifinals, one of the most memorable

Champions League matches between these two clubs took place. In three weeks, Barcelona and Real Madrid played each other four times, three in the Champions League and one in La Liga. Matches between Barcelona and Real Madrid in the Champions League continue to captivate soccer fans around the world, showcasing the intense passion, talent, and historical significance associated with this enduring rivalry. The tension and drama on the field were palpable, and Barcelona emerged victorious on aggregate to advance to the final, where they eventually claimed the title.

Champions League Highlights: Spectacular Goals and Dramatic Saves

Throughout its existence, the UEFA Champions League has given us innumerable amazing moments, including magnificent goals and thrilling saves.

Steven Gerrard's Goal (2005): Liverpool was behind 3-0 to AC Milan in the championship game at the half.

Steven Gerrard, the team's captain, spearheaded an incredible comeback in the second half. His goal, a strong header from a cross in the 54th minute, ignited the team's comeback and ultimately resulted in Liverpool winning on penalties.

(2015): In a quarterfinal match between Bayern Munich and Porto, Manuel Neuer made a stunning save to keep Porto from scoring. To stop a close-range header, Neuer lunged to his right. He then quickly stood up and made another incredible reflex save off the rebound, displaying his lightning-quick reflexes.

Bicycle Kick by Cristiano Ronaldo (2018): While playing for Real Madrid against Juventus, Ronaldo scored an incredible bicycle kick goal that astounded everyone. The opposing fans even applauded as the ball crashed into the goal after he soared into the air and executed a wonderfully timed overhead kick.

Keylor Navas' stop (2018): During the Real Madrid vs. In Liverpool's final game, Keylor Navas made a pivotal stop to keep his team ahead. He stopped a striker for Liverpool from unleashing a strong close-range shot by reflexively extending his leg to deflect the ball away from the net and secure a win for Real Madrid.

Free-kick by Andrea Pirlo against Real Madrid in 2005: During the **2005–2006** campaign, Andrea Pirlo demonstrated his dead-ball prowess in a group stage match. Pirlo curled a beautiful free kick from a tight angle on the right side of the field, eluding the Real Madrid wall and nestling into the top corner, leaving the goalkeeper powerless.

The sweeper-keeper role played by Manuel **Neuer in Bayern Munich vs. Juventus in 2016**: *The 2015–2016 season served as a showcase for Manuel Neuer's versatility as a goalkeeper.* Neuer demonstrated excellent poise and agility outside the penalty area during Bayern Munich's Round of 16 second-leg match against Juventus. He made important saves and interventions to keep Bayern Munich ahead of Juventus and move to the next round.

Real Madrid vs. Liverpool, 2018; Gareth Bale's Bicycle Kick: In the championship game of the 2017–18 campaign, Gareth Bale produced an outstanding overhead kick. Bale skillfully connected with a cross while the score remained tied, sending the ball sailing into the top corner. *The goal, which ranks among* *the best in the Champions League, displayed remarkable technique and athleticism* but a few illustrations of the priceless events that have adorned the UEFA Champions League. The rivalry frequently yields breathtaking goals and great saves, leaving football fans throughout the world with unforgettable experiences.

The Champions League's Future

The Champions League, Europe's top club football tournament, has long been a mainstay of the sport. The Champions League will encounter new dynamics and difficulties in the future as the game develops. The Champions League could be expanded to include more clubs as one option. This can entail expanding the pool of participating clubs, adding more qualifying rounds, or even setting up a different competition just for smaller clubs. Increased money and possibly worldwide appeal of the competition would result from an extended tournament. The Champions League's current structure consists of group stages followed by knockout stages. Thoughts have been expressed regarding changing this framework. One suggestion is to implement a league-style system where teams play more games against various opponents, generating more income and possibly lowering the possibility of top clubs being removed early.

The Champions League's future will continue to be greatly influenced by financial considerations. There might be more pressure to strike a balance between the interests of the top clubs and the footballing world at large. To ensure a more equitable distribution and lessen the widening economic gaps between clubs, the distribution of prize money, TV rights, and commercial revenue could be changed.

The Champions League enjoys a huge global audience, and UEFA may look for ways to increase its reach. This can entail holding matches in several nations or even organizing regional editions of the competition to target particular audiences. This expansion might be facilitated by the development of streaming services and digital technology, which would also improve the viewing experience as a whole. Keeping a balance between elite clubs and those from minor divisions is one of the Champions League's ongoing concerns.

To maintain fair competition, UEFA may put in place measures like salary limitations, financial restrictions, or foreign player quotas. These measures might assist in preventing a select group of affluent clubs from continuously dominating the game. We may anticipate big effects from technology as it develops in the Champions League. *Advanced analytics, goal-line technology, and other innovations like video assistant referees (VAR), will probably spread more widely,* improving decision-making accuracy and giving spectators a more engaging experience.

The Champions League is probably going to concentrate on giving fans better experiences because fan engagement is becoming more and more important. This could include programs like interactive broadcasts, virtual reality (VR) experiences, or tournament-related fan events. The ability to link fans and clubs via social media platforms will continue to be vital in fostering more direct relationships.

Printed in Great Britain
by Amazon

38974518R00079